Our Global Village

China

By: Juliana Y. Yuan
Illustrated by: Kathy Mitter

Milliken Publishing Company   St. Louis, Missouri

For my daughters Emily and Adrien so that you will remember your roots— J.Y.Y.

Milliken Publishing Company
1100 Research Blvd.
St. Louis, MO 63132

Editor: Cindy Follman
Managing Editor: Kathy Hilmes

ISBN 1-55863-266-2

A Multicultural Experience

Our Global Village hopes to share ideas, hands-on activities, and resources from other cultures which will lead you, your students, and their families in different experiences. Learning how others live, think, and react is becoming increasingly important. The earth is a global village, and each of us is quickly affected by events, styles, disasters, and ideas from far away. Old barriers of mountains and oceans are disappearing with fax machines and airplanes. It is important to help young children learn about and value the diversity in the world around them. Fortunate is the child who has the opportunity to interact with people who speak different languages, who eat different foods, and whose skins are different colors. This child will come to appreciate the fascinating differences between people in the world while learning that people are much the same. We hope this resource series will help to create a multicultural community in your classroom as you learn and share different languages, customs, and celebrations.

Metric Conversions

The purpose of this page is to aid in the conversion of measurements in this book from the English system to the metric system. Note that the tables below show two types of ounces. Liquid ounces measure the volume of a liquid and have therefore been converted into milliliters. Dry ounces, a measure of weight, have been converted into grams. Because dry substances, such as sugar and flour, may have different densities, it is advisable to measure them according to their weights in ounces rather than their volumes. The measurement unit of the cup has been reserved solely for liquid, or volume, conversions.

Conversion Formulas

when you know	formula	to find / when you know	formula	to find
teaspoons	x 5	milliliters	x .20	teaspoons
tablespoons	x 15	milliliters	x .60	tablespoons
fluid ounces	x 29.57	milliliters	x .03	fluid ounces
liquid cups	x 240	milliliters	x .004	liquid cups
US gallons	x 3.78	liters	x .26	US gallons
dry ounces	x 28.35	grams	x .35	dry ounces
inches	x 2.54	centimeters	x .39	inches
square inches	x 6.45	sq. centimeters	x .15	square inches
feet	x .30	meters	x 3.28	feet
square feet	x .09	square meters	x 10.76	square feet
yards	x .91	meters	x 1.09	yards
miles	x 1.61	kilometers	x .62	miles
square miles	x 2.59	sq. kilometers	x .40	square miles
Fahrenheit	(°F-32)x5/9	Celsius	(°Cx9/5)+32	Fahrenheit

Equivalent Temperatures
32°F = 0°C (water freezes)
212°F = 100°C (water boils)
350°F = 177°C
375°F = 191°C
400°F = 204°C
425°F = 218°C
450°F = 232°C

Common Cooking Conversions
1/2 cup = 120 milliliters
12 fluid ounces = 354.88 milliliters
1 quart (32 oz.) = 950 milliliters
1/2 gallon = 1.89 liters
1 Canadian gallon = 4.55 liters
8 dry ounces, 1/2 pound = 227 grams
16 dry ounces, 1 pound = 454 grams

Table of Contents

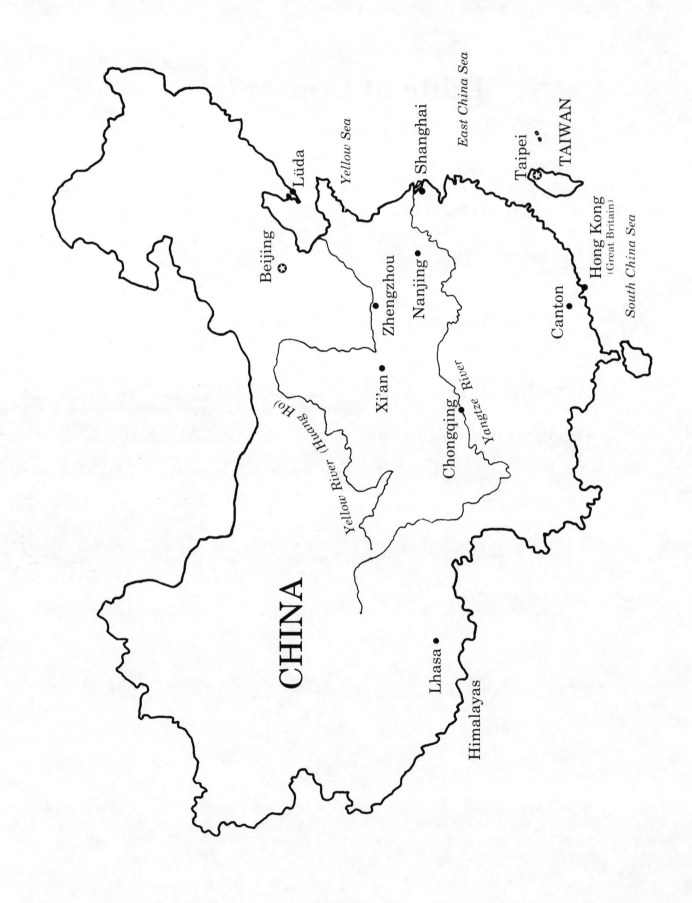

CHINA

Yellow Sea

East China Sea

TAIWAN

Taipei

Shanghai

Lüda

Beijing

Zhengzhou

Nanjing

Hong Kong
(Great Britain)

Canton

South China Sea

Xi'an

Yellow River (Huang Ho)

Chongqing

Yangtze River

Lhasa

Himalayas

China

The western world has always been fascinated by China. China is not only the most populous country in the world, but it also has the longest continuous history of any culture in the world. It is through its long, rich, and carefully recorded history that we are able to cultivate an understanding of the country of China and its people.

Name—Zhong Guo , the "middle kingdom"

Population—The population of China is over 1 billion. 94% of the population is known as HAN (ethnic Chinese), but there are also 55 "national minorities" recognized.

Area—The total area of China is 3,696,032 square miles (9,572,723 square kilometers). There are 21 provinces and 5 autonomous regions.

Major Rivers—The two major rivers in China are the Yellow River (Huang Ho) and the Yangtze River.

Climate—China's climate is primarily temperate, but it varies from bitterly cold in the north to tropical in the south.

Most Populous Cities—China's two most populous cities are Beijing, the capital of China, and Shanghai.

Language—Mandarin is the official dialect of the country, although there are many dialects which vary from region to region.

Physical Features

The land mass of China ranges from the Himalayan Highlands to the Pacific Ocean. It is subject to a variety of climates; from desert in the west to coastal in the east, from subpolar in the north to subtropical in the south. Rainfall is sparse in the far west, low to moderate in the northeast, and heavy in the south.

A number of major river systems cut through the land mass, carrying the water and silt necessary for agriculture. However, due to an uneven rainfall distribution, the rivers have also presented age-old problems in China such as the need to facilitate irrigation in the north and prevent floods in the south.

China is slightly larger in size than the United States. The two countries are located almost equally within the north–south range along the equator, but China has more land areas that are unproductive and uninhabitable, and its climate varies at greater extremes than the climate in the United States. Cultivated land area in China is about 70% of that in the United States.

In Your Classroom

Bring a globe or a world map to the classroom and have the children locate China. Then have them locate the United States, and compare the two countries in terms of size.

Identify the equator and compare the two countries in terms of their locations along the equator. Locate the two major rivers in China and the Himalayan Mountain Range—the tallest mountain range in the world.

A History Of China

China's history can be traced back to at least 2000 B.C. The origin of China's modern day written language has been found cast in ancient bronzes and inscribed on tortoise shells and bones.

Two great philosophers who left their teachings deeply ingrained in Chinese society were Confucius and Lao Zi. They lived during the 6th century B.C. Confucius stressed the importance of family and education—the basis of Chinese society. Lao Zi founded the religion of Daoism which stressed beauty in nature. The Chinese love for nature stems from the teachings of Lao Zi and can be found throughout the Chinese arts.

The first emperor of China, Qin Shi Huang Di (221–210 B.C.), unified the country. He was responsible for the building of the Great Wall along the northern borders for defense against nomadic tribes. The Great Wall still stands today and is the longest structure ever built. It is the only man-made structure that can be seen from outer space.

China's history is divided into dynasties. When a new group came into power, the new emperor would proclaim a new dynasty. Some dynasties were short-lived, with only one emperor, while others lasted for hundreds of years, with as many as 16 emperors. China was not always ruled by Chinese emperors. The Yuan Dynasty (1279–1368 A.D.), for example, was ruled by the Mongols, a nomadic tribe from the north. Kublai Khan was the first emperor of this dynasty, and it was during his reign that Marco Polo and other westerners came to the new capital city of Beijing, which is still the capital of China today.

In 1912, the imperial government ended, and China became a Republic under the leadership of Sun Yat-sen. In 1949, the Communist party, headed by Mao Zhe Dong, took over mainland China and established The People's Republic of China. In opposition to The People's Republic of China, Chiang Kai-shek and his supporters settled on the island of Taiwan and established The Republic of China.

Inventions and Discoveries

China has made many contributions to the world in art, science, and technology.

Chinese Inventions

silk
the compass
paper
wood block printing and the first
    moveable type
gunpowder
stirrups and horse collars
the wheelbarrow
canal locks
paper money
the kite
porcelain
the folding umbrella

Chinese Discoveries Introduced to the West

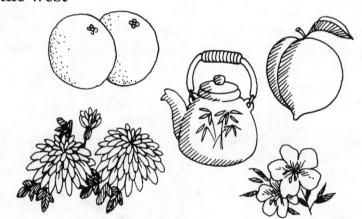

peaches
apricots
oranges
grapefruit
tangerines and other citrus fruits
tea
chrysanthemums
peonies
camellias
azaleas

In Your Classroom

Discuss the various inventions and discoveries made by the Chinese. How do they affect our lives today? Which inventions are the most important and/or significant? Why?

Language

The Chinese do not use an alphabet as we do to produce the sounds of their language. Instead, each Chinese word is called a **character**, and each character represents an idea or object but does not indicate how the word should be pronounced or what it sounds like.

The written form of Chinese was standardized around 200 B.C., but spoken Chinese has never been standardized. As a result, there are many dialects spoken in China. Sometimes a person from the southern part of China cannot understand a person from the northern part of China; however, both can communicate with each other by writing down the characters.

Chinese characters are really pictures of things (**pictographs**) or pictures of ideas (**ideographs**). There are thousands of characters that make up the Chinese language. The following are some examples of modern Chinese characters and how they were derived from ancient pictographs:

	Ancient	Modern
Sun	☉	日
Moon	☽	月
Mountain	ᨈ	山
Field	田	田

If we put the pictograph for the sun, 日 , and the moon, 月 , together, we get 日月 , an ideograph meaning "bright."

Some other examples of ideographs:

Dawn 旦 Sun over the ground.

Up 上 Something growing above the ground.

Down 下 Something growing under the ground.

In Your Classroom

Have a native Chinese person come visit your classroom and give spoken examples of several Chinese dialects. This will give your students an idea of how the Chinese language sounds, as well as the difference in sound between dialects.

Below are several more ancient pictographs. How do these pictographs look like the words they represent? Compare them to the modern characters that have been derived from them. Do the characters still look like a picture of the word they represent? Have students make up some pictographs of their own for various objects in the classroom.

	Ancient	Modern
tree	木	木
earth		土
water		水
ox		牛

Have a Chinese calligrapher come into your classroom and demonstrate how the Chinese characters are drawn. Have the calligrapher write each child's name in Chinese, and let the children tape them to the tops of their desks.

**Use the Language chapter in conjunction with the calligraphy section in the Creative Arts chapter of this book. Calligraphy is the art of the Chinese written language.

Daily Life

Family

There is a saying in China: *The older one is, the more respected. The younger one is, the more adored.* The family is the most important unit in Chinese society. Confucius taught that everyone in a family must behave properly towards one another. In his teachings, he emphasized that if children obeyed and respected their parents, then, as adults, they would respect authority. This would, in turn, allow the whole country to be harmonious and at peace. The virtue of respect towards one's elders is known as **filial piety**, and it is one of the most important rules of behavior in Chinese culture.

Every member of the family is clearly identified by his or her title in Chinese. Family members are not as clearly identified in the United States. For example, the word "brother" in English could mean either older or younger brother, and the title "grand-mother" does not distinguish between maternal or paternal heritage. In China, a title clearly identifies the position of the relative. Following are some examples of family titles: (Spellings below are phonetic. Pronounce **g** as in **g**o, **Wai** like **why**, and the **e** in **ge ge** as in **the**, versus the long **ee** sound in **dee dee**.)

Mah mah	Mother
Bah bah	Father
Jieh jieh	Older sister
May may	Younger sister
Ge ge	Older brother
Dee dee	Younger brother
Po po	Grandmother (father's side)
Wai po	Grandmother (mother's side)
Gung gung	Grandfather (father's side)
Wai gung	Grandfather (mother's side)

Aunts, uncles, and cousins are also identified by their titles, which indicate their order (whether older or younger) and lineage (whether paternal or maternal).

Customs Practiced in Celebration of Newborns

By Chinese custom, a child is instantly considered to be one year old at birth. A year later, the child is considered two years old. After the birth of a child, the proud father gives out eggs that have been dyed red, just as cigars are often passed out after the birth of a child in the United States. However, no further celebration is held until the infant is one month old. Due to the high infant mortality rate of times past, celebrations were put off for a month to assure the health and survival of the infant. After a month, a banquet is held for family members and friends. The newborn will also receive his or her first "red envelopes" containing good luck money from all the honored guests. Red is the color for happiness and is used for births, weddings, anniversaries, the new year, or any festive occasion.

Education

Education in China has always been held in high esteem. Confucius is considered the patron of teachers, and teachers are regarded with great respect and honor. Throughout Chinese history, all of the important government and official positions have been held by well-educated people. Thus, education is associated with a good job. A prestigious job not only means monetary security, but also brings honor to one's family.

Chinese Manners

Showing respect towards others is one of the principle virtues in Chinese society, and it is the basis for many rules of etiquette and proper behavior. For example, both hands should be used when handing an item from one person to another, as well as when accepting an item. An older person can use one hand when giving an item to a child; however, a child should never accept an item from an elder using only one hand.

When one receives a gift, it is considered rude to open the present right away. The gift should be put aside and opened after the giver has left.

The words **syeh syeh** (phonetic spelling), meaning "thank you," are probably the most important words Chinese children are taught to say, just as the words "please" and "thank you" are stressed in America.

In Your Classroom

Have the children identify their siblings using the four Chinese terms: "jieh jieh," "may may," "ge ge," and "dee dee."

Have the children give objects to and receive objects from each other with both hands. Practice saying "syeh syeh" as one accepts the object.

Have children discuss the roles and importance of their various family members.

Foods

Because of the wide range of climates in this vast country, there are varying food products found in the different regions of China. In nothern China, where the climate is colder, the main crop is wheat, so breads and noodles are the main staples. In southern China, where the climate is warmer and wetter, rice is easily grown and is the main staple there.

Vegetables are the next most consumed foods. They are often eaten fresh, or they are salted and pickled in countless ways as a means of preserving them for the winter months.

Meat is eaten in small quantities and is often used to flavor the food with which it is cooked. Fruits are eaten for snacks and are sometimes served as dessert.

Soups are served as the first course in the south, as the last course in the north, and during the meal in some central regions.

Recipes

Fried Rice

2 cups cooked rice
1 egg, beaten
2 scallions, chopped
2 slices of bacon, diced
1 tbsp. soy sauce

Scramble the egg in a little oil and set aside. Cook the bacon thoroughly and do not drain the grease. Add the scallions and stir-fry briefly. Add the rice and stir-fry, breaking up any lumps. Add the scrambled egg, continue to stir-fry, and add the soy sauce.

This recipe can be easily multiplied to desired quantity.

Cold Peanut Butter Noodles

Spaghetti or Chinese egg noodles, cooked and drained.

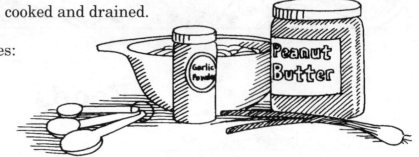

Sauce for 1 large serving of noodles:
1 tsp. creamy peanut butter
1 tbsp. hot water
1 tbsp. soy sauce
1 scallion, chopped
garlic powder

Thin peanut butter with the hot water and soy sauce, and pour over the cooked noodles. Toss with chopped scallion and a sprinkle of garlic powder.

Cucumber Salad

2 cucumbers, halved and finely sliced
2-3 tbsps. soy sauce, according to taste
1 tsp. vinegar
1 tsp. sugar
1/2 tsp. sesame oil (optional)
dash of salt

Toss all ingredients together just before serving.

Almond Float

1 envelope unflavored gelatin
1/3 cup cold water
3/4 cup boiling water
1/3 cup sugar
1 cup milk
1 tsp. almond extract
1 can fruit cocktail

Soften gelatin in cold water, add boiling water and sugar. Stir thoroughly until dissolved. Pour in milk and extract. Put in a square cake pan and chill until set. Cut into 2 inch cubes, and add the can of fruit cocktail with syrup.

In Your Classroom

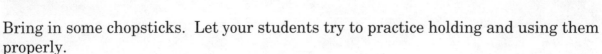

Chopsticks

Bring in some chopsticks. Let your students try to practice holding and using them properly.

To Use: Hold the chopsticks roughly in the middle with the larger end on top and the smaller end on the bottom to pick up the food. Rest the upper part of one of the chopsticks against the area between your thumb and index finger on the palm of your hand. Rest the lower part against your ring finger. This chopstick stays firm when eating.

Hold the other chopstick with your thumb, index, and middle fingers of the same hand. This one will be on top and will be the one to move to pick up the food.

Keep the two bottom ends even as you try to use them for eating. Good luck!

Try eating your various recipes with chopsticks. Try picking up the cucumbers and grains of rice with them.

Serve hot tea made from tea leaves instead of tea bags. Watch the leaves sink to indicate when the tea is ready.

Discuss the differences and similarities between Chinese food and American food, and how the foods are cooked and served, i.e., stir-frying versus deep frying, and roasting.

Ask your students if any of them have ever eaten in a Chinese restaurant and have them describe the experience. Discuss how their experiences might compare or contrast to eating a real Chinese meal in China.

Creative Arts

Porcelain

The Chinese discovered the art of making fine porcelain, or "china," named after its country of origin. Porcelain is a type of pottery made of clay and other minerals. The secret mixture for porcelain produced pottery as thin as egg shells. Much of the pottery made from porcelain, or "china," was highly admired by the West, and great quantities were made and exported to Europe and the United States.

Silk

Another art form discovered by the Chinese is the making of beautiful fabric from silk. This fine, light material is made from spinning fibers produced from the eggs of the silkworm. The Chinese knew how to produce silk as early as 1500 B.C. This fabric was highly sought after and desired by the people of many countries—India, Persia, and as far west as Rome during the time of Christ.

Painting and Calligraphy

Painting and calligraphy are considered the two greatest artistic achievements of the Chinese. Interestingly, both art forms are created with the same instrument and medium—brush and ink. The Chinese written language is made up of pictographs, pictures of things, and ideographs, pictures of ideas, so it is fitting that both paintings and the "pictures," or Chinese characters, are created with the same brush and ink.

Part of the technique of calligraphy is knowing how to hold the brush. It is held firmly between the thumb and the index and middle fingers of your hand. The other two fingers are held lightly behind the brush to keep it balanced. The brush is always held completely vertical which allows for full use of its tip.

                                           China

In Your Classroom

Obtain a bamboo brush from any art supply store and a bottle of India ink. Dip the stiff brush in water until it is soft and pliable. Pour some India ink into a dish. It is very dark and concentrated; you may use it full strength or dilute it with some water. Experiment with varying the ink tones. Practice writing the Chinese numbers from 1 to 10. Use the India ink carefully; it is a permanent dye, and it stains!

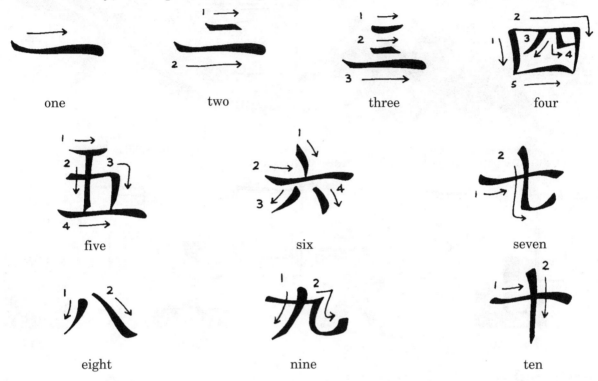

one	two	three	four
five	six	seven
eight	nine	ten

With the same brush and ink, try to paint some pictures. Use the tip of the brush for delicate strokes and press harder on the brush for bolder, heavier strokes.

Examples:

A very popular art form practiced by people of all ages is paper cuttings.

Make stencils of half of each of the following designs and have the children trace them on the fold of a sheet of paper. Then have them cut and unfold for the finished product.

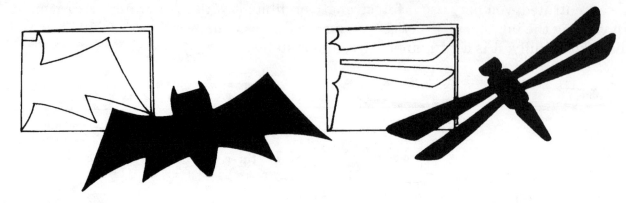

They can also cut out the following Chinese characters:

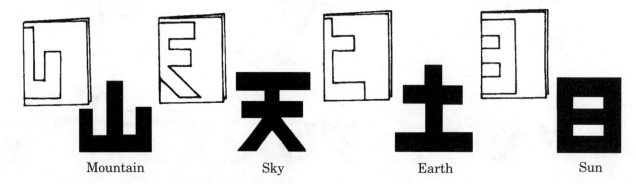

| Mountain | Sky | Earth | Sun |

Favorite Subjects in Chinese Art

In Chinese art, there are certain subjects or motifs that are very popular and have been used for centuries in all forms of art such as painting, jade carving, decoration on porcelains, and embroideries. The following are some of the more frequently used motifs and what they symbolize.

Bamboo—This is an emblem of strength and durability. The bamboo will bend with the wind, but does not break easily. It is associated with spring because of its tender green leaves and new shoots.

Lotus—This flower symbolizes purity and perfection. The large blossoms rise out of the mud in shallow water but remain pure and beautiful. This flower is associated with summer when it is in full bloom.

Chrysanthemum—This is generally associated with retirement and a life of ease. Just as the flowers bloom in autumn, late in the year, so too, should a person enjoy the beauty of life in his or her "autumn" years.

Plum Tree—This represents strength and long life. The blossoms appear on leafless and gnarled old trees in late winter. The plum tree is associated with winter.

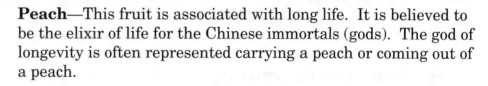

Peach—This fruit is associated with long life. It is believed to be the elixir of life for the Chinese immortals (gods). The god of longevity is often represented carrying a peach or coming out of a peach.

Crane—This bird is one of the most popular symbols of long life and is often placed with a pine tree. The pine tree is also a symbol of long life and strength since it remains green all year.

Bat—The bat is the emblem of happiness and wealth. Contrary to the image that comes to mind when we think of bats, bats in China are depicted in art as very colorful and decorative creatures, looking more like butterflies than bats.

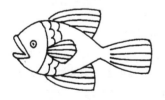

Fish—The fish represents wealth and abundance. It symbolizes abundance of food or abundance of children in a family.

In Your Classroom

Visit an art museum and locate the gallery or galleries where Chinese art objects are on display. Look at the paintings, porcelains, and any other objects, and try to locate some of the motifs discussed above.

Check out books on Chinese art from your school or local library, and again notice and discuss the repeatedly used subjects and motifs.

Festivals and Celebrations

There are innumerable festivals and celebrations that vary from region to region in a country as old and large as China. However, there are a number of major festivals that have a long tradition and are celebrated with much enthusiasm and excitement throughout the country.

Ching Ming Festival (Spring)

Chinese families traditionally remember their ancestors on this occasion in spring when the air is fresh and the sky is clear and sunny. The words **ching ming** mean "pure and bright." An elaborate picnic is brought to the family grave site and before each dish is served, it is placed for a moment on the altar stone of the chief ancestor.

In Your Classroom

Invite parents and grandparents to come to class and share a story about a deceased ancestor.

Dragon Boat Festival (Summer)

This festival is celebrated on the fifth day of the fifth month. It is also known as "Poet's Day" in commemoration of the famous poet, Chu Yuan, who lived several centuries before Christ. It is a day of kite flying and watching dragon boat races. **Dragon boats** are wooden boats that are long and narrow with a carved dragon head on the bow. Twenty oarsmen row to the beat of a drummer in each boat. A special treat called **jung** is eaten during the week of the Dragon Boat Festival. It is made of a sticky rice with a sweet bean or meat and vegetable filling, wrapped in taro leaves and held together with string, and steamed.

Moon Festival (Autumn)

This celebration takes place on the fifteenth day of the eighth moon, when the moon is at its fullest. The festivities take place outside at night so that everyone can admire the full and bright moon. Children make or buy colorful paper lanterns in the shapes of animals, flowers, and fruits. Candles are placed inside the lanterns, and the children carry their lanterns on sticks and parade about. When darkness falls, the lanterns glow like little moons dangling from their hands. Rich pastries with sweet fillings such as lotus seed or red bean paste are called **moon cakes** and are enjoyed by everyone during this time of year. Next to the Chinese New Year, the Moon Festival is the most popular and widely celebrated of Chinese Festivals. It brings the same excitement to the children that Halloween does in the United States. This festival is also known as the Mid-Autumn Festival.

In Your Classroom

Buy some accordion lanterns from a novelty shop, and tie them onto wooden chopsticks with string. Have the children parade around the school. If there is a Chinese grocery store in your area, buy a few moon cakes. (They are very rich and expensive!) Cut the moon cakes into small pieces for the children to sample.

Chinese New Year (Winter)

The Chinese New Year is the most festive and joyous of all the celebrations. The New Year begins on the 20th day of the first moon which may fall anywhere between January and March. It provides a break from the cold and monotony of winter. In the old days, preparation began weeks in advance, and festivities lasted a full month after New Year's Day from the new moon to the full moon. The families would plan and prepare large meals for the celebration. About ten days before the New Year, families and businesses begin sweeping away the old year by cleaning out their houses and shops. Artists paint new poems on red paper for people to place in their homes and shops. Large branches of plum blossoms are bought to decorate the homes much like Christmas trees in the West.

On New Year's Eve, family members gather together for a feast and to welcome in the new year. Firecrackers explode to frighten away evil spirits and to celebrate joy and happiness. New Year's Day is a time for remembering ancestors and for visiting close friends and relatives. The children wait in anticipation to see who will stop by and bring them red envelopes filled with good luck money. **Lion dances** are performed in the streets to bands of gong and drum players, accompanied by more explosions of firecrackers. Lion dances are processional-like dances in which a person parades underneath a hand-crafted lion or dragon head and other people often trail behind with its body made of colorful streamers. (See illustration on p. 20)

Some objects commonly seen during the Chinese New Year include:

—pairs of long sheets of red paper with four character couplets, or poems, on them. They express best wishes and good fortune for the coming year.

—red envelopes with gold characters. Good luck money is placed inside and given to children and young adults during this time, much in the same spirit as Christmas and Hannukah presents.

—flowers. The two flowers most associated with the New Year are the plum blossom and the water narcissus. Plum blossoms represent hope and courage. They are the earliest blossoms to burst forth at the end of the cold winter, and they are associated with the entire season of winter. The water narcissus also blossoms at this time. If the white flowers blossom exactly on New Year's Day, then good fortune is believed to continue throughout the new year.

—oranges and tangerines. These citrus fruits are in season during the winter months and are symbolic of good luck. They are frequently displayed in homes and stores.

—togetherness trays. Trays with eight compartments, each filled with a special treat of dried fruits, sweetmeats, and candies, are set out to welcome guests and relatives who stop by.

In Your Classroom

Make a field trip to a local Chinese grocery store during this time, and try to find some or all of the Chinese New Year objects listed above.

Make envelopes out of red construction paper or any other type of paper, and place play money inside for exchange. You can also buy a pack of red envelopes from the Chinese grocery; they are relatively inexpensive.

Buy a few paper white narcissus bulbs from a nursery, fill a bowl or tray with pebbles or rocks, pour water over the rocks, and place the bulbs on top. It's great fun to watch the bulbs grow and blossom. Continue to water occasionally. Do not let the bowl become completely dry.

The Chinese Zodiac

The Chinese have an astrological zodiac chart based on a cycle of 12 animals. Below is a diagram of the chart. Have the children locate their animal sign based on the year in which they were born. Then read the personality traits associated with that animal. Birth years provided below date from 1910, so children can look up the signs of their grandparents and parents as well as their own. Though the years labelled below end with 1993 at the sign of the Rooster, they continue in sequential order, clockwise around the chart (i.e., 1994—DOG, 1995—PIG, and so on).

PIG
1911-1923-1935-
1947-1959-1971-
1983-

RAT
1912-1924-1936-
1948-1960-1972-
1984-

DOG
1910-1922-1934-
1946-1958-1970-
1982-

BUFFALO
1913-1925-1937-
1949-1961-1973-
1985-

ROOSTER
1921-1933-1945-
1957-1969-1981-
1993-

TIGER
1914-1926-1938-
1950-1962-1974-
1986-

MONKEY
1920-1932-1944-
1956-1968-1980-
1992-

RABBIT
1915-1927-1939-
1951-1963-1975-
1987-

GOAT
1919-1931-1943-
1955-1967-1979-
1991-

DRAGON
1916-1928-1940-
1952-1964-1976-
1988-

HORSE
1918-1930-1942-
1954-1966-1978-
1990-

SNAKE
1917-1929-1941-
1953-1965-1977-
1989-

MONKEY—You are very intelligent, clever, and well-liked by everyone. You will have success in any field you try.

ROOSTER—You are a hard worker and definite in your decisions. You are not afraid to speak your mind and are, therefore, sometimes boastful. You will make a good restaurant owner, publicist, or world traveler.

DOG—You are honest and faithful to those you love, but you tend to worry too much and find fault with others. You will make an excellent business person, teacher, or secret agent.

PIG—You are a good friend because you are sincere, tolerant, and honest, but by expecting the same from others, you may be terribly disappointed. You will thrive in the arts as an entertainer, or you may make a great lawyer.

RAT—You are imaginative, charming, and very generous to those you love, though you do have the tendency to be quick-tempered and overly critical. You will be happy as a writer, critic, or publicist.

BUFFALO—You are a born leader, and you inspire confidence in those around you. Be careful about being too demanding. You are also methodical and good with your hands. You will make a good surgeon, general, or hairdresser.

TIGER—You are sensitive, emotional, and capable of great love, but you tend to be stubborn about what you think is right. You will make an excellent boss, explorer, or race car driver.

RABBIT—You are affectionate, cooperative, and always pleasant, and people like to be around you. You can, however, get too sentimental and seem superficial. You will make a successful business person, lawyer, diplomat, or actor.

DRAGON—You are full of life and enthusiasm and a very popular individual with a reputation for being "funloving." You will make a good artist, priest, or politician.

SNAKE—You are wise and charming. You are also romantic and a deep thinker, but you tend to procrastinate and be a bit stingy about money. You will make a good teacher, writer, or psychiatrist.

HORSE—You are an amazingly hard worker and very independent. Although you are intelligent and friendly, you can sometimes be a bit selfish. You will find success as an adventurer, scientist, or poet.

GOAT—You are charming, elegant, and artistic, and you like material comforts, but you also have a tendency to complain about things and worry a bit too much. You will make a good actor, gardener, or beachcomber.

Toys and Games

Children of all countries and all ages share a universal love for games and play. Games can be as simple as marbles or as complex as checkers. There are a number of toys and games that children in China can make themselves with everyday objects. A game which has become the national sport of China is **ping pong**, now an English word. The following are some toys and games found all over China.

Ti Jienzi

(pronounced: tee, jee-en ze), or kick shuttlecock

To make the toy you will need:

1 square piece of cloth about 6" x 6"
2 tbsp. dried rice or beans
a washer or coin the size of a 50¢ piece
3 feathers (from any craft shop)

Place the coin onto the center of the cloth, put the dried rice or beans on top, tie all the corners and edges of the cloth up tightly with the rubber band, and insert the feathers.

To play, drop the shuttlecock onto the side of your foot and kick it up into the air. Try to keep the shuttlecock (**jienzi**) bouncing in the air with the side of your foot as long as possible.

Zhuazi

(pronounced: jwa ze), or "grab game," a Chinese version of jacks

You will need:

2 pieces of cloth about 5" x 5", smaller for smaller hands
dried rice or beans
a needle and thread
10 small pebbles or other small hard objects

To make the beanbag used in zhuazi, sew the sides of the two pieces of cloth together, making sure that the stitching is tight. Leave a small opening, and fill the bag with dried beans or rice. Sew the small opening closed.

To play, pick up the pebbles with both hands, and shake them out onto the floor. Using only one hand, toss the bag up into the air. While it is up, pick up as many of the pebbles as possible, then catch the bag again before it falls to the ground. If the bag falls to the ground, the player loses his or her turn, and it becomes the next player's turn to try.

Eagle Chases the Baby Chicks
(a Chinese version of tag)

To play, one child is the eagle, and the other children are the chicks. The children who are chicks form a chain by grasping each other around the waist from behind. The child in front, leading the chain, is the mother hen. The emphasis is on the group staying together under the protection of the mother hen. They are given a ten count head start before the eagle tries to catch the "baby chick" at the end of the line. The chicks must hold on to one another and follow the lead of the mother hen, whose job it is to watch the eagle and keep her chicks away. If the end chick is tagged by the eagle, then it must leave the chain.

Paper, Scissors, and Rock

Two children sit facing each other, each holding out a fist. On the count of three, each child will either form a rock by keeping the fist, form paper by opening the fist, or form scissors by extending the index and the middle fingers. The rock can smash the scissors, the scissors can cut the paper, and the paper can wrap the rock. So, the rock wins over the scissors, the scissors win over the paper, and the paper wins over the rock. Continue to count to three, and see which hand sign wins each time. If both hands hold out the same sign, then it is a tie.

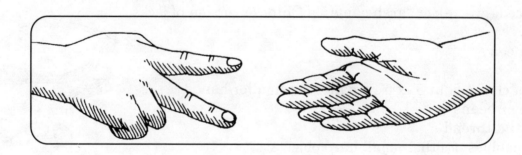

Additional Resources

Books for Children

Cheng, Hou-tien. *The Chinese New Year*. New York: Holt, 1976.

Fawdry, Marguerite. *Chinese Childhood*. New York: Barron's, 1977.

Harris, Peter, trans. *Monkey and the Three Wizards*. Scarsdale, NY: Bradbury, 1977.

Hitz, Demi. *Under the Shade of the Mulberry Tree*. Englewood, NJ: Prentice Hall, 1979.

Kendeall, Carol, and Yao-wen Li. *Sweet and Sour: Tales from China*. London: The Bodley Head Ltd., 1978.

Preston, L.E. *Ching's Magic Brush*. Minneapolis, MN: Carolrhoda, 1973.

Van Woerkom, Dorothy. *The Rat, the Ox and the Zodiac*. New York: Crown, 1976.

Waters, Kate, and Madelina Slovenz-Low. *Lion Dancer: Ernie Wan's Chinese New Year*. New York: Scholastic, Inc., 1990.

Williams, Jay. *Everyone Knows What a Dragon Looks Like*. New York: Four Winds.

Wyndham, Robert. *Chinese Mother Goose Rhymes*. New York: Putnam, 1982.

Yolen, Jane. *The Seeing Stick*. New York: Crowell, 1977.

Young, Ed. *High on a Hill: A Book of Chinese Riddles*. New York: Philomel-Putnam, 1980.

Zimelman, Nathan. *I Will Teach You of Peach Stone*. New York: Lothrop, Lee & Shepard, 1976.

Resources for Teachers

Chinese Cultural Activities. Vols. 1 and 2. N.Y. A.R.T.S., 32 Market St., New York, NY 10002.

Christie, Anthony. *Chinese Mythology*. Middlesex, England: Hamlyn House, 1968.

Gascoigne, Bamber. *The Dynasties and Treasures of China*. New York: Viking Press, 1973.

Green, Sandra Aili. *Chinese Festivals and Customs*. PEASE, University of Michigan, Ann Arbor, MI, 1980.

Goldstein, Steven, Kathrin Sear, and Richard Buck. *The People's Republic of China: A Basic Handbook*. 4th ed., New York: The Asian Society, Inc., 1984.

Henson, Martha, and Laqueta Barstow. *An Introduction to Chinese Folklore*. Center for International Studies, University of Missouri-St. Louis, MO, 1986.

Joseph, William, A., ed. *Global Studies: China*. Guilford, CN: Dushkin Publishing Group, Inc., 1987.

Lewis, John. *The Chinese Word for Horse and Other Stories*. New York: Schocken Books, 1980.

Martin, Roberta, ed. *China: A Teaching Workbook*. 2nd ed., East Asian Curriculum Project, East Asian Institute, Columbia University, NY, 1983.

Myrda, Jan. *The Silk Road: A Journey from the High Pamirs and Ili Through Sinkiang and Kansu*. New York: Pantheon, 1980.

Motomatsu, Nancy, ed. *China: A Book of Activities*. KNOW-NET Dissemination Project, Seattle School District, WA, 1984.

Newman, Richard. *About Chinese*. New York: Penguin Books, 1971.

Polo, Marco. *The Travels of Marco Polo*. New York: Penguin Books, 1981.

Shoresman, Michele, and Roberta Gumport. *A Children's Palace: Activities about China for Elementary Students*. Center for Asian Studies, University of Illinois, Urbana-Champaign, IL, 1986.

Sullivan, Michael. *The Arts of China*. Berkeley: University of California Press, 1979.

Ancient China. The Great Age of Man Series, vol. 17. New York: Time-Life Books, 1967.

White, Caryn. *Play Chinese Games*. East Asian Outreach Program, Yale University, New Haven, Connecticut, 1985.

For additional resources on China, contact a university with a Center for Asian Studies.

A partial listing:
Columbia University, New York, NY; University of Illinois, Urbana-Champaign, IL; University of Michigan, Ann Arbor, MI; University of Missouri-St. Louis, St. Louis, MO; University of Washington, Seattle, WA; Yale University, New Haven, CN.

Notes

Notes